أنا جونْ وأنا أركبُ جرارةَ
أبي عبرَ الحقول.
هيا نذهبْ!

My name's John. I'm riding through
the fields on Dad's tractor.

**Rumble-grumble
judder-trundle!**

Let's go!

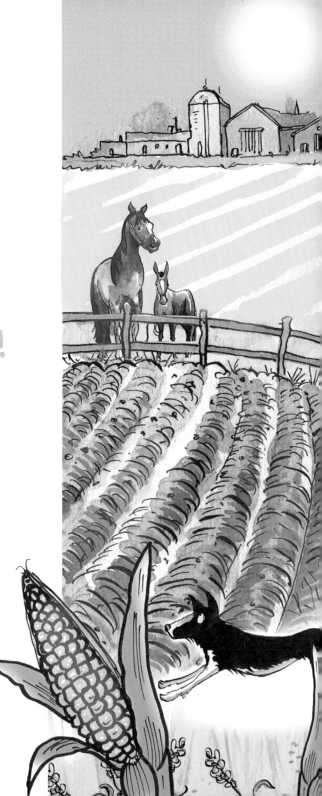

Julie Kingdon
Illustrated by Leo Broadley

Arabic translation by Wafa' Tarnowska

Mantra Lingua

أنا ليانْ و أنا أركبُ وراءَ أبي
على الدراجة.
هيا نذهبْ!

I'm Lian and I ride on the
back of Daddy's bicycle.

bring

briiing!

Let's go!

إسمي فالدا وأنا منطلِقةٌ وراءَ
أختي على الدراجةِ الثلجية.
هيا نذهبْ!

I'm Falda and I'm whizzing along
on my big sister's snow-mobile.

Vrmmm Vrmmm
Varrooooom!

Let's go!

إسمي لوسيا. أنا وأبي نركبُ
قاربَ الجندولِ على الماء.
هيا نذهبْ!

My name's Lucia. My daddy and I glide
through the water in his gondola.

Splash splish swoosh swish!

Let's Go!

أنا سيرا، وأنا أغطُ على الماءِ
بطائرةِ خالتي البحرية.
هيا نذهبْ!

I'm Sera and I'm landing on the
water in my aunty's seaplane.

Niiiaaaw woosh judder judder judder **Sploosh!**

Let's go!

إسمي ليزي. انا و أختي
نركبُ سيّارةَ الأُجرة.
هيا نذهبْ!

My name's Lizzie. My brother
and I are riding in a taxi.

beeeep

beeeep!

Let's Go!

اسمي نيرانْ وأنا راكبةٌ دراجةَ
التوكتوك التي يملكها عمي.
هيا نذهبْ!

I'm Niran and I'm riding home
on my uncle's tuk-tuk.

Honk honk

bounce brake!

Let's go!

إسمي توميلو. أستطيعُ أن أطيرَ مع أمي في طائرةِ الهيليكوبترْ.
هيا نذهبْ!

My name is Tumelo. I can fly with my mum in her helicopter.

Swish swish whirr vrrrum!

Let's Go!

أنا ماساكْ وأنا أسرعُ في الثلجِ على
مزلجةٍ يشدُها كلاب الهاسكي.
هيا نذهبْ!

I'm Massak and I'm zooming across the
snow on a sledge pulled by huskies.

Woof woof
whiiiiiiiizzzzzz!

Let's go!

اسمي أربانْ وأنا مسافرٌ عبرَ
البلادِ في القطار.
هيا نذهبْ!

My name's Arpan. I'm travelling
through the country on a train.

Clickerty

clickerty

clackerty

Whoooooooooooooosh!

Let's go!

أنا زاهورْ وأنا أركبُ دراجةَ
أبي النارية.
هيا نذهبْ!

I'm Zahur and I'm riding
on my dad's motorbike.

PHUT PHUT

VVRRRRROOOOOOM!

LET'S GO!

Thailand

South Africa

Norway

India

Italy

UK

Russia

China

USA

Egypt

Fiji